A Bible Reference About Angels and Demons

With Comments on Good and Evil

Robert A. Munroe
1968, reformatted in 2021

Note: This is not a theological or religious work, but a literature compilation by a layperson with comments and should be considered informative but not authoritative.

Foreword

There is a lot of things this theme is not: it's not written by an expert of a person trained in theology and/or religion, it's not complete, it's not objective (free from personal or denominational bias), it's not written with a detail that allows the reader to trace every word to a reference source.

However, with proper guidance from a trained person or member of the clergy it can be used as a background source or discussion source for adults interested in the broad subjects of angelology, demonology, and evil. It is I believe more comprehensive than any number of reference sources studied because it integrates those sources, and no one source had all the Biblical passages noted for a particular interest. Some of the passages were not mentioned in any reference examined and were found by the author during reading; the angel in white in Daniel 12:6 for example.

The source for the Biblical text and quotations, unless otherwise noted, was from the Revised Standard Version of the Holy Bible. Quite a few references to evil are from the King James Version of the Holy Bible the source of many Protestant ideas on demonology. The apocryphal data, admittedly valuable for this work was unfamiliar to the writer and not considered part of the Bible by his church;

therefore, the serious student should pursue this area.

The object of the theme was to document some Biblical and classical background on the general subject of the devil (Satan) in the Old Testament (OT). As readily can be seen the subject did not break cleanly at the OT so I continued into the New Testament (NT). The devil had a number of names as did God, the meaning of the noun and verb Satan became a pursuit in itself, and each of the major religions had many intelligent thoughts on the subject. It soon developed that since the 14allegedly used to be an angel, the nature of angels had to be examined, and creation stories reviewed since God made everything. The question than arose, "If God made everything, then did He make evil?" That was pretty hard for a layperson to understand, especially since by this time he was getting in pretty deep.

In the area of evil, the author failed miserably to remain objective since he was very involved by this time. The rest of the subjects are as objective as possible, and if anything may be too academic and cold. The coldness and dullness will go away by reading the Biblical references and getting involved yourself. If nothing else, the material should be thought provoking and the reading of every reference in this theme will accomplish a considerable amount of scriptural ground.

Since the Roman Catholic Bible differs from the RSV in the OT, some of the references may be out of place. A serious attempt was made to normalize all passages back to the RSV for a baseline. If something is out of place, please consult more expert sources. Many of the referenced sources will not seem applicable to the subject since the sources used by scholars are translated into the Bible we read, and some of the comments go back to the older Hebrew, Greek, Aramaic, and Latin texts.

Several sources were used to research this theme, using the library at Harpur College at the State University of New York - Binghamton, which has many Biblical reference books. Not all the source investigated are listed here, such as the many concordances as they did not address any of the subjects in sufficient depth or add anything to the larger collections of the source material.

Source Material Used:

Interpreter's Dictionary of the Bible (1962), Abingdon Press

Interpreter's Bible (1952) Abingdon Press

The Theology of the Old Testament, A. B. Davidson, (1904), Scribner & Son

Jewish Encyclopedia, Isidore Singer (ed), Ktav

Universal Jewish Encyclopedia, Isaac (ed), Universal Jewish Encyclopedia Co. (1943)

New Catholic Encyclopedia (1967), McGraw-Hill

Encyclopedia of Bible Creatures, Moller-Christensen, V. and K. E. Jordt Jorgensen, Fortress Press

Encyclopedia of Religion and Ethics, Hastings and Selbie, Kessinger Press

Revised Standard Version of the Bible

King James Version of the Bible

Collier's Encyclopedia, (1958) Collier Publishing

Three sources form the overwhelming majority of the theme material: they are 1, 5, and 8.

Table of Contents

Discussion on Our Outlook Today

Do We Believe In Demons and Angels?

In our alleged sophisticated world today are there signs of demonology? I believe there are signs although we may not readily admit it.

For example, if one buys an automobile or appliance and it continually breaks down even if repaired by a competent mechanic or technician we may determine it is "jinxed" or a "lemon". In some states there are even "lemon" laws to protect consumers. That is an indication that we believe there is a non-physical explanation that forces beyond our control are the cause. That is a belief in evil or demons.

I went to college with an US Air Force veteran who told of a transport plane that was always having a problem with engine failures despite having engines replaced and with different crews flying it. Crews came to believe it was "jinxed". My college roommate flew in that plane from Iceland to Newfoundland with military women and children along with household goods. Crossing the Atlantic they had one engine after another of the four engine plane fail. They threw out household goods to lighten the load and when they were down to two engines the airmen were told to don parachutes and be prepared to jump to lighten the load so the plane might make land. Jumping into the cold north

Atlantic would be certain death. Luckily they made the coast and as they were making an emergency landing one of the two remaining engines failed. Everyone made it safely, but convincing the passengers and crew that the plane was not jinxed was not possible.

Have you watched a baseball game and seen fans wear their hats in funny positions to make a rally happen? Is that not a ritual to change fate? I am not sure why that happens in baseball and not football, but it does. If we read about a story like that in the Bible we would have an example of a magic ritual affecting an event and changing a course of action (is that evil)? As the Budweiser beer advertisement says, "It is only weird if it doesn't work". The statement implies sometimes magic works.

People around us often characterize bad luck as the evidence that something untoward is happening and is not "normal", and in ancient times the cause would be assigned to evil forces, the result of sin, or demons. I would assert that today we have changed the language but have not changed our basic thinking in that we want to assign a cause and have substituted luck for evil.

Ancient people did not think as we do today and the concept of ideas in our head or our thinking was existent. Everything was external to them so mental illness was thought to be the result of demons or evil forces. When they consulted statues or mummified bodies of gurus those statues and bodies "talked to them" and were consulted by priests in many cultures. Thus there are often stories of demons and evil spirits even in the New Testament. Jesus most certainly would know that there was something we call mental illness today, but I suspect that in order to relate to his audience he had to use examples of externalization to demonstrate his curing of those illnesses.

In Luke 8:33 we see that Jesus had the demons go from a man into pigs on a far hillside and the pigs jumped off the steep bank and were drowned. This indeed is not natural as pigs can swim well. It was a demonstration I think of Jesus using a physical event that the people of the time could understand.

In Genesis 32:22-31 Jacob wrestles with a stranger that ends up being God and God rewards him. This is a story that was in the ancient world before the OT was written. I believe Jacob wrestled with the situation he found himself in and struggled with that problem in his mind as we do today and reached the conclusion that God wanted him to do. Have we not "wrestled" with a problem and gone to God in prayer? The word for wrestle is used repeatedly in both the Old and New Testaments. Psalm 13:2 "how long must I wrestle with my thoughts" which is a reflection of internalization of the struggle.

Sometimes we use expressions that have a history of demon causations, There is a German expression when a person gets a spasm or "stitch" in their side and it is called a hexenschuss which is a witches shot or arrow. When someone sneezes we might exclaim "Gesundheit" which literally means health but has been interpreted as a blessing or even "God bless you" to some.

As you read further in Section 6. Aversion of Demons we still do rituals, wear special colors, and behave today as we did in past millennia in our church services. We might say it is tradition, but and observer could fairly say it is superstition. If nothing else, I hope that this reading will make the reader more aware of some of our customs and use that awareness when reading the Bible.

Bells are rung in the sanctuary in some services or incense is burned and this to ward off evil spirits or demons. The use of the colors purple or blue are often used in clothing or decorations as those colors were hard to dye cloth in ancient times and so were reserved for royalty or priests.

Abaddon

The word means the "nether land". Other interpretations are; "abode of the dead," "the pit," "slough of the despond," "the nether Abaddon of darkness," and in rabbinic literature the third lowest stratum of the earth reserved for the wicked.

References: Psalm 88:11, Job 26.6, 28:22, 31:12, Proverbs 15:11, 27:20

Apollyon

Revelation 9:11, "They have as king over them the angel of the bottomless pit; his name in Hebrew is Abaddon , and in Greek he is called Apollyon." Another translation of the text, substitutes the "Destroyer" for Apollyon. We see that in the New Testament (NT) the king of the pit has become synonymous with the pit. The locusts referred to in Revelation 9:11 are derived from the parallel story in Joel 1:4.

Beelzebub (alternate spellings are Beelzebul, Bealzebub)

In the OT the name meant Lord of the Fly and was an idol of the Philistine City of Ekron. The oracle of Beelzebub is consulted by the king of Israel (Ahaziah) in 2 Kings 1:2. It is believed that the change in meaning came about because the Aramaic vernacular spoken by Jews at the time of Christ had changed the 'zebub to 'debub which meant enmity or hostility. In the NT it came to mean the same as Satan or "chief of the devils".

The Latin Vulgate connects the Old Testament (OT) and the NT through 2 Kings reference, but others believe that the reference in the NT is to Baal, a heathen god. In post biblical Hebrew and Syriac the latter part of the word means dung, and the reference is to the Lord of Dung which is repeated in the apocryphal book "Ascension of Isaiah" and German folklore. In the Dead Sea Scrolls and OT usage it is accepted to mean Satan, Belial, Samael. A word Bizbah is used in Mandean literature, and the Iranian word bazah- bat means "lord of sin".

References: Matthew 10:25, 12:24-27, Mark 3:22, Luke 11:15-19

Belial

The word literally means "un-worth". In most OT usages it has been translated to something different in the RSV, but in many cases the word is used directly in the King James Version (KJV). Sons or daughters of Belial are "base fellows," and alone the word is sometimes used to denote an uncouth person. The witness of Belial means to give false testimony. The rivers of Belial are currents of adversity compared to the rivers in the nether world. The counselor of Belial is a plotter of evil.

The NT uses of Belial use the word in context found in the apocryphal literature, which is the Prince of Evil thus equal to Satan. The word seems similar to Druj the Iranian Spirit of Deceit. The Dead Sea Scroll called the Zedokite or War Document describes a war between the Sons of Light and the Sons of Darkness. The Sons of Light won, the defeating

Belial. The Sons of Light are described as the tribes of Levi, Judah, and Benjamin.

References: Sons or daughters of Belial; Deuteronomy 13:13, Judges 19:22, I Samuel 1:16, 2:12, 20:1, 30:22, Proverbs 16:17, Used alone; I Samuel 23:6 and Job 34:18. Vicious hoax or rumor Deuteronomy 15:9, Psalm 41:9, Psalm 101.3. False witness; Proverbs 19:28. Counselor of evil; Nahum 1:11. Rivers of Belial; 2 Samuel 22:12 and Psalm 18:4. Evil power; Nahum 1:14 and Hosea 1:10. Prince of evil; 2 Corinthians 6:15. Man of lawlessness; 2 Thessalonians 2:3.

Demons

The subject of demons or daimons or evil spirits is so involved that the following outline was taken from the Interpreter's Bible Dictionary. The outline is followed by comments on each item supplemented by other source material.

The Old Testament

    Daimonism

    a. daimon b. spirit

    Demoniacal possession

    "Demons" as a generic term

    Specific demons

        Lilith

Resheph

the midday demon

the vampire

the faery arrow

the terror in the night

Catastrophe (De'bher)

Qete

the seven evil spirits

the king of terrors

Azazel

The habitat of demons

Aversion of demons

Apocryphal and pseudopigraphic literature (omitted in this theme)

In the New Testament

Pagan deities as demons

Demons as noxious spirits

Expulsion of demons

Names of demons

Daimon

This is the Hebrew equivalent of demon. In old literature, daimon is translated "god" thus a man of god. It meant the same as a sudden flash or insight or inspiration.   A man of gods in Greek or Hittite literature was a seer.

References: Deuteronomy 33:1, 1 Samuel 2:27, 9:6, 1 Kings 13.1, 17:18, 2 Kings 4:7, and Psalm 90:1.

In later literature the word takes on a different meaning. In Genesis 30:8 when Rachel gave birth to Naphtah it describes her as wrestling with her sister Leah as if possessed by a daimon which is an apt description of birth for many women. Balaam showed his ability to prophesize dependent on an encounter with a god, and is possessed in Numbers 22:38.

Spirit

The words daimon and spirit are used almost interchangeably in the early literature.

The word spirit is used in Numbers 24:2 the way daimon was in Numbers 22:38. In 2 Samuel 1:9 Saul's wound is described as a sickness caused by possession by a spirit, translated in the RSV as "anguish". In the OT there are references to evil spirits sent by God, and the spirit was used to describe a gifted man. Guidance or protection by personal angels is written using both daimon and spirit.

During these early times a spirit could also mean the breath escaping from a dying man and leading to an un-embodied personality, or it could mean the wind. We have all heard of the expressions "good wind" and "ill wind" which originate from Near East religious thought. A monotheistic religion subordinates spirits and daimons to a central figure (God) and makes them angels or envoys.

References: spirit = daimon: 1 Samuel 10:10 and 1 Samuel 19:23. Evil spirit sent by God: 1 Samuel 16:15-16, 16:23. Guidance by personal daimon: Exodus 23:23, 32:23. Guidance by personal spirit: Isaiah 63:14, Psalm 143:10. A gifted man described by spirit: Exodus 31:3, 35:31.

Demoniacal Possession

The early writings are really attempts by ancient peoples to describe their emotions by externalizing them. We describe emotions today as from within a person, the ancients tended to describe them as upon a person. For example, aspiration becomes inspiration, ecstasy becomes rapture or a state of being seized, and insight becomes revelation. An ecstatic man is one on whom spirit has leapt, and terror is an outer control over inner self. Excitement is a blow from an outer spirit, and desire is due to an outer blow.

This whole concept of externalizing emotions is quite common in Sumerian literature of the period. The Akkadian demon for desire had the name of Ahhasu. The suffering servant in Isaiah 53:4 is described as being "smitten by God" and has a parallel in the Hittite literature where the god (Siunas) is compounded to Siuniyahh to mean visited with sickness. The Arabs use a term called "Jinn-struck" for demented, which is similar to our modern term of awe-struck and love-struck (which may not be far from demented).

The Bible is not absolutely clear whether spirit is that which affects or is that which is effected.

References: Ecstatic man: Judges 14:6, 1 Samuel 10:6, 11:6. Terror in man: Exodus 15:14, Job 21:6, Psalm 48:7, Isaiah 34:14. Excitement: Judges 13:25, Psalm 77:5. Desire: Exodus 9:3, 2 Samuel 1:9.

Demons as a generic term

The word demon is used in the OT to describe objects of pagan worship cultivated by recalcitrant Israelites, ("heathen deities"). The winged bull or colossus (Akkadian sedu) is described in post Biblical exilic literature as a malign or protective daimon. The word is also used to describe "hairy ones," satyrs, ostriches, wild beasts, hyenas, goats, he-goats, and wild goats. This is similar to Arab beliefs.

Specific demons

Demons survive as a figure of speech today, even if we do not believe in them. We speak of gremlins when describing an unknown fault in a machine for example. Demons are not supposed to be the personification of evils, but the forces that cause them. Today we may say, "A cramp has seized me". In 2 Samuel 1:9 we see that the term "anguish has seized me" was used. The problem in Biblical interpretation is to distinguish between the event physically or to assume that, "anguish" is the name of a specific demon.

Lilith

The name appears in Isaiah 34:14 and has an Akkadian female counterpart known as Lilitu, that was supposed to have tempted men in sexual dreams. Through the years Lilith has become confused with Lamashtu who is a child stealing hag. Isaiah identifies her with unclean birds and ghoulish beasts (kite, pelican, owl, wildcats, and jackals). A child stealing wolf was known as a bogey-wolf. Thus see that our bogey-men and bogey-wolfs are around 3,500 years old. I wonder if the modern Lilith society of women understand the source of the name.

Rasheph

This Canaanite god of plague and pestilence appears in the Bible and the literature of Mari, Ugarit, Zenjirli, Karatape, Cyprus, Carthage and others from 1800BC to 350BC. She appears in Egyptian writings as far back as the Late Middle Kingdom. In Habakkuk 3:5 she is paired with another god (De'bher) catastrophe, as attendants to God when he takes to war, which is parallel to the ancient belief that major gods went to war with a pair of bodyguards.

In Job 5:7 the ancient texts use the word to express the fact that a man is born to trouble and that it surrounds him and seems even to jump up from the dust of the ground itself, an idea seen several times in non-Biblical texts. Resheph is identified with birds of carrion like the vulture.

References: Deuteronomy 32:24, Psalm 76:3, Psalm 78:48, Songs of Solomon 8:6

The midday demon

In Psalm 91:6, this demon is responsible for the overpowering noonday heat that often resulted in sunstroke for the people traveling or living in the desert. The Greek god Pan was named by ancient Greeks as being responsible for the terrible heat of the noon.

The Vampire

This demon is mentioned in Proverbs 30:15 and is described as a demon with two greedy and insatiable daughters. Some Jewish sources use the translation "horse leech". The Arabic, Aramaic, and Syriac words mean leech or limpet, while the Arabic specifically means vampire or ghoul.

The faery arrow

There are many instances in ancient literature where disease or misfortune is attributed to darts or shafts from demons. In the Iliad, Apollo inflicts plague by shooting darts. In English folklore sick people have been described as elf-shot.   A Cyprus document around 340BC describes Resheph, the plague god, as "Resheph of the arrow". The reference is Phoencian.

References: Job 6:4, 34:6, and Psalm 91:5, 7:13.

The terror in the night

This demon is a counterpart to the faery arrow (Psalm 91:5) but works in the night. In the Songs of Solomon 3:8 the men friends of the bridegroom are armed against "alarms of the night," which is probably the same demon. It is universal that weddings have escorts to guard against demons. In Isaiah 34:14 we have the "night monster". The night demon is similar to the Akkadian demon, muttalik musi, the "night stalker".

De'bher (Catastrophe)

This demon appears in several places associated with Resheph the faery arrow and the midday demon. The name derives from a Hebrew root meaning "cast prone," used in Psalm 18:47 and 47:3.

References: Psalm 91:5-6 and Habakkuk 3:5.

Qeteb

The Hebrew root means "cut off," and is similar to the Sumerian demon of plague, Namtar known all over Mesopotamia. This demon is not found in any English translations by direct name that I am aware of, but has been woven in with interpretation of verse. It is essentially used to parallel catastrophe.

References: Deuteronomy 32:24, Psalm 91:6, and Hosea 13:14. 4

The seven evil spirits

In Deuteronomy 28:22 the Israelites are warned to follow the commandments of God or suffer the seven evil spirits which are: 1. Consumption, 2. Fever, 3. Inflammation, 4. Fiery Heat, 5. Drought, 6. Blasting, and 7. Mildew. These seven evil ills or demons are parallels to the seven Mesopotamian demons of plague and pestilence that acted as agents for the god of disease, Ira.

The king of terrors

In Job 18:14 the "king of terrors" is implied as the demonic king of the nether world or Sheol. This is comparable to the pagan god Nergal in Babylonian mythology, know as the "King of the Terrible Place". In Vergil's Georgica IV, p. 469 the word meaning "is brought" is translated literally to, "Thou mayest well bring him" implying solemn and ceremonious occasion. The story is that the wicked man vying for social advancement reaches his goal and is finally presented at court...the court of Hades!

Azazel

Literally translated the word means scapegoat, but it is generally accepted that in ancient days it referred to as "he-goats" or wilderness demons. A closer translation of the Hebrew may be "hairy ones". The usage was made to describe the demons or satyrs inhabiting wastes, ruins, and the desert at night. It is similar in concept to the Arabic Jinn. Leviticus 17:7 prohibits their worship as heathen deities.

References: Leviticus 16:8, 16:10, and 16:26

The habitat of demons

Islamic, Arabic, and Iranian literature note that demons occupy areas such as deserts, ruins, wastes, and it should not come as a great surprise since those areas are hostile to man today. In ancient Semitic folklore the desert and sea were scenes of primordial chaos and thus were even more frightening. In the NT Jesus is tempted in the desert thus continuing the OT.

References: Leviticus 16:10, Isaiah 13:21, 34:14, Luke 4:1-2, and Matthew 12:43

Other demons

Before continuing with our outline presented on pages 6 to 9 several other demons will be addressed.

The OT understanding is one who destroys the relationship between God and men, especially Israel. This is accomplished by leading men to sin, accusing them before God, and seeking to defeat God's plans. The term is definitely not identified with the ruler of this world, but secondary implications are of evil desire, fallen angels, and angel of death.

The apocryphal references are interesting as they affected our thinking through history, and influenced NT writings. The Book of Enoch, Wisdom of Solomon, Asmodeus, Tobit, Mastema, Book of Jubilees, Samael, III Baruch, and the Ascension of Isaiah carry references to the devil. The Wisdom of Solomon 2:23-24 identifies the serpent of Genesis 3, which is repeated in the NT. The origin of demons is traced to Genesis 6:1-6 by the Book of Enoch.

Devil

In the NT the devil generally appears as a single, supernatural, adversary of God that tempts and leads men astray. He is described as the ruler of this world, the prince of the world, and among other things he is named as having the power of death.

References: Tempter: Matthew 4:1, 12:17, 13:19, 13:39, Luke 4:1, 8:12, 1 Thessalonians 3:5, 1 John 2:14, John 8:44, 13:2, Acts 10:38, Ephesians 4:27, 6:11, 6:16, 1 Timothy 3:6-7, 2 Timothy 2:26, James 4:7, and 1 Peter 5:8. Devil or devils child: John 6:70, 8:44, 1 John 3:8, and 3:10. Power of death: Hebrews 2:14. Ruler of this world: Matthew 25:31, Jude 9, Revelation 2:10, 12:9-12, 20:2-10, Ephesians 2:2, Mark 3:22, John 12:31, 14:30, 16:11, 2 and Corinthians 4:4. OT adversary: Revelation 12:10. Implied in Romans 8:33-34. Used as adjective: 2 Timothy 3:3, and Titus 2:3. As a verb: Luke 16:1. Jesus healed those possessed by the devil: Acts 10:38. The works of the devil were destroyed by the Son of God: 1 John 3:8.

Some of the terms used to describe the devil in the above references are: "prince of demons" Mark 3:22, "prince of this world" John 12:31, "prince and power of the air" Ephesians 2:2, "tempter" Matthew 12:17 and 1 Thessalonians 3:5, "the serpent" 2 Corinthians 11:3, "old serpent" Revelation 12:9 and 20:2, "evil one" Matthew 13:19, Ephesians 6:16, and John 2:14, "father of lies" John 8:44, "disguised as the angel of light" 2 Corinthians 11:14, "Apollyon" Revelation 11:11.

Dragon (sea monster, sea serpent, Rahab, Leviathan)

Several references are made in the dragon theme to an alleged primordial battle between God and a draconic monster variously styled as; Leviathan Job 3:8, Psalm 74:14, Isaiah 27:1; Rahab Job 7:12, Habakkuk 3:8; sea monster Job 7:12, Psalm 74:13, Isaiah 51:9; sea serpent Psalm 68:22-23.

Lucifer

The name Lucifer literally means "light bearer" and was the name of Venus the morning star, and has been used to refer to Satan before his fall from heaven. In Isaiah 14:12 the king of Babylon is referred to in a story misunderstood by many to be the devil. The king of Babylon had boasted that he would ascend to heaven and exalt his throne above the stars of God and then descend to Sheol. Luke 10:18 refers to this fall as exemplifying the power of God over demons.

Revelation 9:1 mentions a star falling from heaven to earth and being given the key to the shaft of the bottomless pit. The fall of a dragon after a fight with Michael and his angels is described in Revelation 12:7-9, which is believed to be the same fall described in all of the above discussion.

Satan

The Semitic word satan meant to oppose or hinder, and as a noun meant opposer or adversary. It is used a number of times in the OT, but only three times as a noun in a superhuman sense.

References: Superhuman personality; 1 Chronicles 21:1, Job 1, 2, Zechariah 3:1. As a verb; Zechariah 3:1, Psalm 38:21, 71:13, 109:4-20-29. Noun in a human sense; 1 Samuel 29:4, 2 Samuel 19:22. It appears in a human sense involving an angel; Numbers 22:22, 22:32. God raised up adversaries in a human sense; 1 Kings 11:14, 11:23, and 11:25.

In the NT the word Satan takes on a continual meaning as a super human adversary of God, in competition for men's souls. Satan's fall from heaven, his identification with the serpent of old, his connection with the Devil, and suggestions are made to deliver people to him.

References: Superhuman; Romans 16:20, Matthew 4:10, 12:26, 16:23, Mark 1:13, 3:23, 3:26, 4:15, 8:33, Luke 4:8 (KJV), 10:18, 11:18, 13:16, 22:3, 22:31, John 13:27, Acts 5:3, 26:18, 1 Corinthians 5:5, 7:5, 2 Corinthians 2:11, 11:14, 12:7, 1 Thessalonians 2:18, 1 Timothy 1:20, 5:15, Revelation 2:9, 2:13, 2:24, 3:9, 12:9, 20:2-7, and 2 Thessalonians 2:9.   People given to Satan; 1 Corinthians 5:5, and 1 Timothy 1:20. Satan's fall;

Luke 10:18. The serpent. Devil, and Satan are one; Revelation 12:9 and 20:2.

Aversion of Demons

We have to be careful not to laugh too loudly at this practice of the ancient people, as we whistle in the dark, sing to ourselves, and use our noisemakers at New Year's Eve parties. It is a very old custom to ring bells or in other ways make noise to scare demons away. Bells were sometimes attached to priest's robes, and in Exodus 28:35 the ringing of bells precedes the high priest entering the holy of the holies. It is believed the blowing of the ram's horn at the first of each month, and at special occasions, is a carry over of making noises to scare demons away. Specific instructions are given in Leviticus 16:12-13 for fumigation of the high priest to expel demons at the start of the agricultural year.

The blue cord on the high priest's robes in Numbers 15:38 is supposed to keep the demons away, in the original use according to some sources. An ancient Hittite-Hurrian story concerns a mother who gave her son, Kessi, a piece of blue wool as an amulet when he went hunting. It was a custom in Germany within the last 120 years to put a piece of blue thread around the lock of the house door after the birth of a child to keep out evil spirits. Some sources indicate the story of Kessi as the reason for dressing boys in blue; boys being the important children.

In Deuteronomy 6:8, Exodus 13:16, and Proverbs 7:3 frontlets or writings are mentioned which at God's command tell what should be worn. In Deuteronomy 6:9 and 11:20 the same command is given, but to write the words and attach them to the doorposts of their houses which Jews do to this day. Amulets at God's command?

A recurring source of demons

Before we go into the NT it would be well to review a source of many OT and NT demons, the Babylonian Creation Epic learned by the Jews during the exile. On page 7, the description of dragon and references fits the ancient conception of Tiamat the Babylonian god. In the NT the references stick to serpent for the most part. See Psalm 74 for a creations story based on this source. In 2 Samuel 22:9-11, God is described like a dragon with fire from his mouth and smoke from his nostrils! (see Psalm 18 also) In the Babylonian Creation Epic, Apsu and Tiamat were male and female deities begetting gods with Tiamat pictured as a dragon. Apsu is slain by Ea his offspring. Tiamat after an epic battle (primordial chaos ?) is slain by Marduk, Ea's son. Marduk is declared chief god, and he fashioned the world (Kingu) from Tiamat's remains and fashioned mankind from her blood. Marduk was named as three gods in one; god of earth, god of nature, and god of the universe. The influence of this story is felt through out the OT and NT on books written after the exile, and especially the NT book of Revelation.

Another source of demons and stories was Egypt. Egyptian theology at Memphis is said that the god Ptah was creator of all living things, which came into existence from   what his heart and lungs commanded. Egyptian theology at Elephantine said the god Khnum fashioned all living things from clay on a potter's wheel (Genesis 2:7?).

Early theologians were split on literal interpretations of Genesis 1:26. The Antiochian school was pro and the Alexandrian school con with Augustine fluctuating between the two.

References: Biblical references to creation or God's power of creation are; Jeremiah 27:5, 31:35, Genesis 1, 2 and 14:19, Psalms 18, 33, 104, and 147, Proverbs 3:19, Isaiah 41:4,

41:20, 45:7, and 55:11.

Apocryphal and pseudopigraphic literature (omitted in this theme)

In the New Testament

The NT conception of demons is nearly identical with apocryphal and pseudopigraphic literature, the Dead Sea Scrolls, and early strata of the Talmud. The Iranian cultural influence is definite and differs from the OT.

To quote from page 822 of the Interpreter's Bible

Dictionary, "As in Iranian teaching and in the Dead Sea Scrolls, the faithful, it is held, belong necessarily to the 'children of light' and are thus part of the army of God, supported by him and his angels against the prince of darkness. But they are armed also by the special redemptive power communicated to his apostles by the incarnate God. The authority of the Godhead with which he was himself invested when he walked among them as the Son of Man, is transmitted by grace to those diffusers of his message; and the unclean spirits must needs obey it, once it is invoked against them Moreover, the subjection of men to demons is   itself merely the result of their own refusal to accept redemption and of their own obstinate disobedience of God's law".

The above view is not too different from Augustine's view on evil which is covered later, and demons are personifications of evil to most of us.

Pagan deities as demons

There are several references in the NT to worshipping idols, pagan gods, and the like. However, Acts 17:18, 1 Corinthians 10:20, and Revelation 9:20 refer directly to the worship of demons. They probably allude in a general sense to Isaiah 65:11 since the Canaanite gods Fortune and Destiny are considered demons.

Demons as noxious spirits

Noxious means harmful to the health or well being,

and there are many references in the Bible to many afflictions, physical and mental, as being caused by spirits; an ancient idea. With modern medicine we know that this basic idea has much merit, also. The NT refers to men possessed, cripple, mad, and sometimes a combination of possessed and diseased. A slightly different term moon-struck (lunatic in KJV) appears in Matthew 4:24 and 17:15.

Acts similar to the Talmudic "spirit of catalepsy" in; Luke 8:29, Acts 5:16, and 8:7. A man possessed in; Mark 9:18 and Luke 4:33. Physical disorders described in; Matthew 4:24, 8:16-28, 9:32, and 12:22. Mark 9:18, Luke 11:14, and 13:11. Psychic disorders are shown in; Matthew 11:18, Luke 4:33, and John 10:19-21. Both demoniac and disease in; Matthew 4:24, Mark 1:32, Acts 5:16, 8:7, and 10:38.

Expulsion of demons

Demons are expelled by invoking the name of God in several books of the Bible.

Nowhere does the NT original language include a verb "exorcise" or "expel by conjuration" to describe Jesus's casting out of demons. The verb is used in Acts 19:13 to describe the unsuccessful attempt by Jewish exorcists or magicians. The Samaritans misinterpreted Numbers 6:27 as an amulet.

Names of demons

See Abaddon, Apollyon, Beelzebub, and Belial on page 14, Devil on page 26, dragon, Lucifer, and Satan on pages 28 & 29. The Destroyer in 1 Corinthians 10:10 is understood, by some scholars, to be an avenging angel; not a malign spirit or demon. This thought is similar to the destructive angel of 2 Samuel 24:16. However, if this view is correct than Apollyon of Revelation 9:11 cannot be an angel which is implied by the alternate wording of Destroyer in the RSV. The determination of a spirit being an angel or demon is decided by the criteria that an angel is an agent of God, and a demon is a rebel against God.

Note very carefully that whether or not the angel does man evil or ill in man's sight has nothing to do with the determination, since an evil spirit in the Bible does not infer morality.

Anti-Christ

The anti-christ is addressed here because in some quarters the anti-christ has been solely the Devil, which is not that simple in Biblical literature. The concept of an anti-christ is attributed to both Persian and Babylonian sources. The Persian story concerns the fight between Ahura Mazda (good) and the Angra Malanyn (bad) which allegedly seeped into the NT. However, there is excellent correlation with the Babylonian Creation Epic once again, especially in the NT books of John and Revelation. There is evidence of anti-christ writing in the OT book of Daniel. Several well documented arguments exist that anti-christ Biblical references concern real men of the time the Bible was written.

The book of Daniel was probably written in the Maccabean Age, or around 200BC. The representation in the book of Daniel concerns the Syrian king, Antiochus IV. In the apocryphal literature, Pompey is the anti-christ figure in the Psalms of Solomon.

The Roman Emperor Caligula (37AD-41AD) is supposed to have been one anti-christ figure referenced in the Bible and Jewish apocryphal literature. He is said to have made the Jews put his statue in the Jewish temples as predicted in the book of Daniel. Some recent evidence points to Nero as the anti-christ in Revelation 13:18.

References: Matthew 24:15 and 12:33, Mark 13:14, 2 Thessalonians 2:4, 1 John 2:22 and 4:3, 2 John 7, Luke 11:20, John 12, 14, 16, Revelation 9:1-11, 9:13, 9:19, 111:7, 2:8, 13:1,16:12-16, 17:13-14, and 19:19-21, 2 Corinthians 6:15, and Psalm 18:5.

The idea that God's rule will be manifested over all creatures and the Devil will be eliminated is told in the Jewish document, Testaments of Twelve Patriarchs, written in the Maccabean period. The classical story involves two beasts, as in Revelation, where the four beasts of Daniel's story are in part combined to form one in the beasts in Revelation. The "evil" beasts are given power and authority by the dragon or Devil. One of the beasts is said to represent Rome. The other has two horns like a ram but speaks like a dragon and it performs miracles, deceives people, forces worship of the first beast on penalty of death, and is disguised as the Lamb of God when in truth it is Satanic.

A parallel idea is expressed in Ezekiel 38 and 39 which describes the destruction of the adversary of the Jews, Gog of Magog, by God. The whole concept of the anti-christ, in my opinion, leans more heavily on the Iranian dualism belief (Ahura Mazda vs Angra Malanyn) written in the apocryphal literature than that expected from the majority of Judeo-Christian writings. It is a definitely separate category from the Devil vs. Christ.

Anti-christ, a definition and some history

The Interpreter's Bible Dictionary says, "Strictly defined, a mythical demonic or demonic-human adversary of Christ who will appear before the Second Advent as the last oppressor and the persecutor of Christians, only in turn to be defeated and overcome by Christ in his return to Earth." Legends have appeared in Greek, Latin, Syriac, Coptic, Ethiopic, and Armenian writings.

Persian, and Arabic literature about the anti-christ.

Through history many people or groups of people have been named as the anti-christ by their opposition. Some of these are Mohammedans (Muslims), Saracens, Turks, Jews, Catholic Popes, Protestant Reformers, and more recently; Napoleon, Napoleon III, Kaiser Wilhelm, and Hitler.

Again, quoting from the Interpreter's Bible Dictionary, "For many Christians it is still an important belief, even if the anti-christ is not identified with any actual person, but is considered a supernatural embodiment of evil."

Angels

To make reading easier the outline in the Interpreter's Bible Dictionary will be used once again with supplemental information from other sources added. It seems to me, that the general cleavage between Jewish and Christian source material is that the Jew interprets the language and situation to show that the angel is really a manifestation of God. Also, there seems to be a tendency to "down grade" angels to post-exilic influence and therefore not admit some of the obvious differences from the pre-exilic "angel of YHWH". On the other hand the Christian sources seem to lean towards converting all events despite the period of writing or context, to an angelic "happening" heavily influenced by apocryphal impressions. The reader will have to make up his or her mind, hopefully with the help of clergy. Angel is a messenger or envoy from God; a spiritual being.

In the Old Testament

Angels as messengers

ancient and modern parallels

stories about angels

Angels as celestial beings

ancient Near Eastern parallels

stories about celestial beings

Cherubim and Seraphim

Apocryphal Literature (omitted in this theme)

In the New Testament

Angels as messengers

The Hebrew word for angel is messenger or envoy. In the OT "angels' do many things which will be reviewed here to refresh your memory.

An angel refrained Abraham from killing Isaac
Genesis 22:11

An angel reassured Jacob against Laban's cheating
Genesis 31:11

An angel indicated the character of the burning bush
Exodus 3:2

An angel harbingered the birth of Ishmael
    Genesis 16:7

An angel harbingered the birth of Samson
    Judges 13:3-5

An angel protected Jacob
    Genesis 48:16

An angel escorted the Israelites
    Exodus 23:20-23, 33:2

An angel put a cloud between Egyptians
    Exodus 14:19

An angel invoked a curse against a city
    Judges 5:23

An angel Elijah in the desert
    1 Kings 19:5

Angels inflicted disaster on invaders
    2 Kings 19:35, Isaiah 37:36

An angel protects the faithfull
    Psalm 91:11

Angels rout enemies in battle
    Psalm 35:5-6

An angel is "commander of the army of God"
    Joshua 5:13-14

An angel disappears in the flame of sacrifice
    Judges 13:20-21

Angels possess goodliness or beauty

2 Samuel 14:17, 1 Samuel 29:92 Samuel 19:27

Angels know what happens on earth
    2 Samuel 14:20

Angels eat special food
    Psalm 78:24-25

Female angels with wings
    Zechariah 5:9

These examples are by no means complete, but they should give you an idea of what angels do, and what angels are like.

Ancient and modern parallels

Pagan religions had their messengers also as described in Mesopotamian, Hittite, and Canaanite writings. The Hittite god Hasamilis is described with an event similar to that of Exodus 14:19, where a cloud is put between friend and foe to save the friends. The Mesopotamians believed that, "guardians of welfare" were sent by major gods to protect their followers. Another Hittite text describes good and bad fairies similar to our guardian angels and demons.

The Ras Shamara Texts mention divine messengers as traveling in pairs, an idea reflected in Genesis 19:1. The angel leading the Israelites through the wilderness has a direct counterpart in the Nabatean literature in the form of the deity Shia-alqum, "Accompanier of Peoples," in the OT angels appear especially at wells, besides trees, and in the desert; which is still believed in the Near East for example, the Arabic Jinns and Welis. Angels are described in the Iliad as protecting fighters and eating special food called ambrosia.

References: Exodus 3:2, 23:20-23, 33:2, Genesis 16:7,18:1-2, and 1 Kings 10:4-5 Jewish sources indicate that the Genesis 19 angels were added later than the original texts. Many scholars are in agreement that there is no reference to demons and only one to angels (Deuteronomy 33:2) which reads "holy ones," in the pre-exilic Hebrew writings. "Deuteronomy" by Driver, Edinburgh, published in 1895, page 392 argues that, "holy ones" was not in the original texts.

The first exile referenced Esther 2:6 and Matthew 1:11 was around 598BC. Through out the Bible on of the problems confronting scholars is the time and authorship of passages, so they may assign cultural influences to the writings. A case is made by many that the Babylonian culture and Iranian dualism had a profound effect that is demonstrated by the increase of demons and spirits as time went on.

Stories about angels

Very few stories about angels, if any, are unique or original in that they do not appear in folklore of ancient peoples. For example, the theme of entertaining disguised angels and being compensated for it in Genesis 18:1-10 (Abraham) and Genesis 19 (Lot) has interesting counterparts. In the classical tale of Hyrieus of Tanagra, Hyrieus entertained three gods unaware of their identity and was rewarded with the birth of a son, Orion. Lot's reward for similar hospitality is told in sister versions in both Grimm's collection and Buddhist legend. These storied might have been attempts to get people to be more hospitable, even if promise of reward was not a very moral motivation. However, how many times are we truly altruistic in today's culture?

The example that angels need ladders or staircases to go between heaven and Earth (Genesis 28:12) is seen many times in Egyptian, Greek, Roman, and Indian literature. Ladders were even put in graves to help the souls climb to heaven. The "encampment of holy angels" (Genesis 32:2) is told often in North European folklore and was known as the "ancient host".

From Genesis 32:24-25 and Hosea 12:3-5, we learn that Jacob wrestled with an angel. The same type of story is told in the Odyssey with Manelaus and Proteus the subjects. In folklore it is a common story that a spirit (ghost, fairy, witch, leprechaun, ogre, etc.) must be back in its proper abode by cockcrow, and that the hero gains the special knowledge or magical powers of the spirit when the hero defeats the spirit.

Stories about celestial beings

It is argued that the later poetical books used artistic license or to quote one source "artistic conceit" to recognize a wide range of celestial beings, of the same nature. In the OT some of the names used for angels are; "sons of God", "holy ones", "holy myriads", "sons of the most high", "gods", "sons of the mighty", "heroes", "keepers", "morning stars", "host of the height", "watchers", "princes", "host of the heaven", and "nephilim". References: "sons of God" Genesis 6:2, Job 38:7, Deuteronomy 32:8, Psalms 29:1 and 89:6. "holy ones" Deuteronomy 33:2, Job 15:15, Psalm 89:5-7, and Zechariah 14:5. "holy myriads," Deuteronomy 33:2. "sons of the most high" Psalm 82:6 and Luke 6:35.

Ancient Near Eastern parallels

The term "sons of God" was used in Ugaritic and Canaanite (800BC) literature to describe members of the pantheon. It is argued that these beings are survivors of the pagan deities of more ancient times that become subordinated to the higher YHWH, in much the same way that local numina (pagan city gods), such as Michael and Gabriel, were later made Christian saints. The term "holy ones" was used around 1000BC in Yehimilk texts to describe beings similar to angels. The term "holy ones" is used in the OT to describe pagan gods in some phrases. Some scholars argue that, "sons of God" and like remarks are similar to the upper and lower gods of Mesopotamia, in which case Psalm 82:6-7 and Isaiah 14:14 take on an entirely different meanings.

References: "holy ones" as pagan gods Job 5:1, Psalm 16:3, and Hosea 11:12

More stories about celestial beings

In Genesis 6:1-4 and Psalm 82:6-7 the "sons of God" consorted with human women, and according to some stories this outraged God so much (that the divine spirit would be transmitted to man) that God expelled them from heaven, and limited human life span to 120 years. This theory was built around the ancient belief that intimate contact, especially sexual intercourse, would communicate the qualities from one to another. A cursory glance at the Bible indicates that after Genesis 6 several people are listed as being born and living more than 120 years, if that means anything. A problem exists in timing if we accept that the fall of the angels (including Satan) as noted in apocryphal literature then what was Satan doing in God's court as written in Job?

Two similar story themes exist in folklore concerning gods or the like consorting with humans. One is the Hittite myth of the slaying of the dragon Illuyankas. The other is in Greek mythology that states that intercourse between a divine being and a human results in the death of the human.

In Job 38:7 the sons or God are paralleled with the morning stars (see Lucifer page 28) which appears in Ugaritic texts around 1400BC and before that in Mesopotamian literature. During the last years of the Judean Monarchy the Jews worshipped the stars and were denounced by the prophets in Zephaniah 1:5, Deuteronomy 4:19, and Jeremiah 8:2.

Cherubim and Seraphim

Sometimes it is hard to place the references to the cherubim and seraphim as angels, but for the most part they meet the criteria used here as agents of God. They stand as sentinels at the tree of life, flank the throne of God their images overlaid with gold are set on the ark of the covenant, and God flies through the air on one. Many references to cherubs in ancient literature regards them as sphinx or griffin or winged creatures in Mesopotamian texts around 900BC. In these texts the flying and supporting of thrones is described. The seraphim could be six winged creatures with a serpent in each hand depicted in ancient art. The Hebrew word "seraph" is used in Numbers 21:6-8 for fiery serpents and in Deuteronomy 8:15 and Isaiah 30:6 to describe scorpions.

References: sentinels; Genesis 3:24 and Exodus 28:14-16, flank throne; Psalms 80:1, 99:1, and

Isaiah 37:16. images on Ark; Exodus 25:18-20, 37:6-9, Numbers 7:89, 1 Samuel 4:4, 1 Kings 6:23-28 and 8:6-7. seraphim, cherub descriptions; Exodus 1:4-28 and 10:3-22. seraphim description; Isaiah 6:2-6

One reference specifically on seraphim and cherubim insists they were not angels, but symbols derived from Egyptian griffins found in Egyptian tombs to guard the dead.

The XII Dynasty tomb of Beni Hassan generally agrees with the Biblical descriptions. The seraphim connection with serpents is probably significant as serpents were very important in Hebrew thinking. The Jews worshipped a serpent god to the time of Hezekiah (2 Kings 18:4). A well in Jerusalem is called the Dragon's Fountain in Nehemiah 2:13.

In the New Testament

As in the OT angels performed many duties. These duties include; the harbingering of births, warning Joseph to flee with Mary and Jesus, encouraging Jesus, rolling the stone from His tomb, releasing Peter from prison, and waiting on the throne of God.

References: birth of John the Baptist; Luke 1:11-20. birth of Jesus; Luke 2:8-14. warn Joseph; Matthew 2:13. encouraged Jesus; Luke 28:43. freed Peter; Acts 12:7-10. robed in white linen; Revelation 15:6, 19:4, and Matthew 28:3. bathed in radiance; Luke 2:9, Revelation 18:11, and Matthew 28:3.

The book of Revelation and the book of Enoch (apocryphal) read almost identically regarding the special order of the seven spirits (evidently archangels), and four holy creatures who wait on the throne of God. Both sources also describe four angels, one for each corner of the Earth.

References: Revelation 1:4, 4:5-6, and book of Enoch

Other names are used for angels in the NT; "powers," "elemental spirits of the universe", "spirits," for example. Angels are described as surrounding the throne of God and praising Him. There are allusions to a primeval angelic rebellion against God similar to the described in the OT. The term used in Luke 12:8-9 and Matthew 10:32-33 is believed to be a pious circumlocution for before God, rather than a reference to angels.

References: "powers"; Romans 8:38, 1 Corinthians 15:24, Ephesians 3:10, and 1 Peter 3;22. "elemental spirits": Galatians 4:3 and Colossians 2:8. "angels at God's throne"; Luke 2:13 and Revelation 4:9. "spirits"; Hebrews 1:7. "primeval rebellion"; Jude 6, Revelation 12:7, 16 compare with OT in Job 25;2, Isaiah 24:21, 27:1, and 34;5.

And in case you doubt the whole subject, you should refer to Acts 23:6-8 where the Sadducees denied the existence of angels, spirits, and resurrection. The plebeian Pharisees acknowledged these subjects, and Paul was encouraged in his testimony by a visit from the Lord the following night. The Sadducees were the real sophisticates and intellectuals of the day.

Some Jewish Views on Angels in the Old Testament

The traditional Jewish view appears to differ somewhat in interpretation of language in the OT and what it means. The two main Jewish sources consulted, addressed the subject by looking at it before and after the first exile, therefore before and after a definite Babylonian influence.

Pre-exilic Literature

The major argument is that most references to angels are really manifestations of God, or God appearing to men directly as frequently mentioned in ancient times (ie.

Genesis 18:1). In Genesis 16:7 we see a frequently used term, "angel of the Lord" or "angel of God". The Hebrew is mal'ak YHWH, which is interpreted as a special mission or appearance of God, not a messenger of God's. The argument stems from the Arabic laka and Ethiopic la'aka meaning to go or send a messenger, thus mal'ak becomes a modifier to the word God not a noun by itself. As discussed on page 16, the Jews believe the angels in Genesis 19:1 were added at a later date.

It is argued that besides interpreting many "angelic" events as manifestations of God, that the text reveals that the discussion is really a direct visit by God to man. The Jews argue that the modifier mal'ak used with God, concerning the night long struggle by Jacob with a spiritual being, indicates that Jacob confronted God is used in one instance and angel of God in another to refer to the same event.

References: "manifestation of God"; Judges 5:23, "appearing of God as revealed by text"; Genesis 3:6-9, 3:11, 3:15, 2 Samuel 24:14, and Judges 6:21-23.

We must remember to keep distinct and separate the early Biblical references which read "angel of God" from terms such as "holy ones" which through the years have been interpreted as angels. The term, "angel of God" is a direct connection with God, which is not true with the common usage of terms such as "holy ones". The captain of the Israelite army in the form of a man, is an angel of God. David described as falling into the hand of God that is described in another Book as the hands of an angel of God. Thus the Jewish scholars (and many Christian scholars also) argue that the angel of God is used in pre-exilic Books as another term for God.

References: Numbers 22:22-36, Joshua 5:13-15,

Judges 2:1, 6:21-23, 6:11, 13:3, and 2 Samuel 24:14.

There are several references where the term angel of God is used to praise men. See 1 Samuel 29:9, 2 Samuel 14:17-20, and 19:27. The word mal'ak appears several times to designate special missions of messengers of kings. See 1 Samuel 11:3, 16:19, 19:11, 19:14, 19:20, 1 Kings 20:2, and Jeremiah 27:3.

The angels in Genesis 6:2-4 are discounted as not being in the original texts since they do not appear in any other pre-exilic writings and correlate too well with later concepts, as expressed in folklore and apocryphal literature. The term, angel of God, is used again in Genesis 22:11 and Genesis 28:12 which is altered by a later statement from Jacob, referring directly back to God. The angel of God in Genesis 31:11 is revealed as the God of Bethel in Genesis 31:13, not as an angel. The angel of God in the wilderness (Exodus 14:19) appears as God Himself in Numbers 20:16. An event not as readily explained is noted in Genesis 32:1 where it is implied that the angels of God are described as a company of attendant spirits.

There are a number of references to evil, or similar spirits from God that are not demons (rebels against God), so must be agents or angels, or God Himself. Some references mention lying sprits, God speaking evil, and God surrounded by a host not defined as good or evil.

References: "evil spirits"; Judges 9:23, and 1 Samuel 16:14-16, 18:10. "lying spirit"; 1 Kings 22:19-23

Elijah and Elisha have a number of interesting events surrounding them on this subject. Horsemen in the air are described; Elijah is woken from sleep by an angel, and "an angel spoke to me by the word of the Lord," which might indicate God speaking directly once again, since the expression is unique.

References: 2 Kings 2:12, 6:17, 1 Kings 13:18, 19:5, and 19:7.

The angel of God is named responsible for 185,000 Assyrian army dead which some scholars attribute to a disease divinely delivered. Hosea 12:4 states that Jacob strove with God (Genesis 32:24), implying no difference.

References: 2 Chronicles 32:21, 2 Kings 19:35, and Isaiah 37:36.

In Deuteronomy 32:17 the strange demons or gods are thought to be the equivalent of the Assyrian bull-diety, which is kind of pagan angel if you will. Also, in Deuteronomy33:13 the Hebrew word robeseth is used in the old texts which we translate to couches or choucheth, but the Jews argue is really a reference to a demon. The argument is that robeseth is usually associated with animals and since the poem is making a contrasting comparison to heaven, the word is a personification of the subterranean abyss and its dragon.

Exilic and Post Exilic Literature

In Ezekiel a man described as wearing linen, having a radiant appearance, and acting like a supernatural. Also, is described a spirit similar to the spirit in the hosts of heaven in 1 Kings 22:19-23. However, the spirit in Ezekiel is capitalized to Spirit, and enters into Ezekiel after an appearance "of the likeness of the glory of God". The sounds more like God than an angel. This is repeated several times in Ezekiel and it is argued that these references are really references to God or the Holy Spirit.

References: "supernatural man"; Ezekiel 9:2, 9:5, 40:3, Luke 2:9, and Revelation 18:11 (see page 20). "Spirit" Ezekiel 2:2, 3:12, 3:14, 8:1, and 11:5.

In Isaiah 63:9 a reference is made back to the angel of Exodus 23:20 in a poetical fashion and the word presence or face is used which is most probably borrowed from Exodus 33:11. Some scholars see this as an obvious attempt by the author of Isaiah 63:9 to connect pre-exilic and post-exilic literature.

In Zechariah we see that angels patrol the Earth, have rank, report to the Lord all the Earth, and the top angel is the angel of God, who converses with God. These descriptions act like go betweens (messenger or envoy) between God and man. The angels patrolling the Earth is similar to a term in 2 Samuel, while the rank could be implied in Joshua dependent on interpretation.

References: Zechariah 1:9-19, 5:5, 5:9 (2 female angels), 5:10, 2 Samuel 14:20, and Joshua 5:13-14.

The prologue of Job has not been positively identified as to date of authorship, and some argue that it is older than the rest of the Book. In any case the term "sons of God" in Job 1:6 appear to be the same type of beings written in Genesis 6:2-4 as "beings of the divine order". Note that the story theme still has Satan as a member fo the heavenly court. The theme of God and the heavenly host enticing man or testing man is similar to 1 Kings 22:

God does not trust the "holy ones" even though they are higher than man. Elihu, one of Job's "comforters" refers to himself as an angel, the passage does not mean a supernatural being. A connection with the stars is given once again, where the "sons of God" are teamed with the morning stars; the former shouting for joy and the latter sing. References: 'holy ones'; Job 5:1. "not trusted"; Job 4:18 and 15:15. "Elihu as angel"; Job 33:23. "morning stars"; Job 38:7

In the Psalms there are quite a few references which vary in description and duties.

A listing here indicates that angels;

protect (guardian angel?) 34;7, 91:1 persecute the wicked (Destroyer of the NT) 35:5-6 are evil 78:49 are in council with God 89:6-7 are God's word 103:20-21 are God's host   148:2

There may be another reference to angels in Psalms if one accepts the KJV "makes his angels winds" instead of the more favored RSV "makest winds thy messengers". The reference is 104:4 is believed to be more correct in the RSV language. In Psalm 8:5 David is being praised and the correct wording should probably be "sons of God," not God. The compliment to David is similar to that found in 1 and 2 Samuel on page 67.

The angel of God described in 1 Chronicles 21 is believed to be in reality God in the same sense that the messenger of Ecclesiastes 5:6 was written. Since Ecclesiastes was written first, the assumption is that 1 Chronicles 21 is a copy fo the development in Ecclesiastes.

The book of Daniel contains the story of the angel saving Shadrach, Meshach, and Abednego from fire. Daniel also tells us about Gabriel, and how angels shut the lion's mouths. Daniel refers to the "prince of Greece," "prince of Persia," and the "prince of Israel" that are believed to be guardian angels. For example, in 12:1 we see that the angel Michael is the "prince of Israel". The guardian angels in Daniel are quite similar to the angels described in Isaiah

33:20 believed to be written around 335BC.

References: "angel saving Shadrach"; 3:25, "angel Gabriel"; 8:15-18, "angels shut lion's mouths"; 6:22, "prince of Persia" etc.; 10:12-20, "man in linen"; 12:6

In some of the Books in the OT written at later dates we find that angels (or various descriptors) are subservient to God. There are implications that the host in heaven will or already have been punished after a rebellion against God. References to Rahab, Leviathan, and several other instances reinforce the Jewish argument that the Babylonian Creation Epic show noticeably in post-exilic literature.

References: "subservience to God"; Nehemiah 9:6, Isaiah 40:26, 45:12, Psalm 103:20-21,

"angel rebellion"; Job 25:2, Isaiah 24:21, 27:1, and 34:5. "pagan influence"; Isaiah 27:1 and 51:9, Job 3:8, 9:13, and 26:12-13, Psalms 74:14-17 and 89:10.

Angel of God, Some Comments from Roman Catholic Source

The angel of God appearing so many times in the OT, especially pre-exilic literature is explained by one of more of the following.

Theory a is the messenger is one who therefore speaks God's message in the first person singular as the prophets did, represents the Lord, and transmits His will and promises.

Theory b is the messenger is the ubiquitous God Himself who directly but in human form manifests His message to His chosen leaders.

The messenger is the result of later theological speculation and was interpolated into ancient, naive traditions relating direct nonmediated appearances of God's transcendence and the angel's mediation.

Theory a is accredited to Jerome and Augustine. Theory b is the most popular and it was argued by the early Greek and Latin Fathers of the Church that the angel was a manifestation of the Logos or Christ. This does not differ appreciably from the Jewish views reviewed on page 49.

References: "God Himself appears to man"; Genesis 16:7-13, 21:17-20, 22:11-18, and 31:11-13, Exodus 3:2-6, 14:19, and 14:24-25, Judges 2:1-5, Joshua 5:13-15, Judges 6:11-24, and 13:3-23. "angel perform salvation acts attributed to God" in rest of Bible; Exodus 23:2-232, Genesis 24:7 and 48:16, and Numbers 20:16.

Names of God in the Bible

The Divine Name the "Tetragrammation," was originally written as YHWH, and did not contain any vowels since it was regarded as a too sacred pronoun. The Masoretes added vowels to the name around 600AD to 700AD and indicated that instead of pronouncing the name the reader should use the Hebrew word Adonai meaning Lord or Elohim meaning God. The Greek translators used the word Kyrios (Lord) and the Vulgate used Dominus. Jehovah is a medieval attempt to use YHWH with vowels substituting the J for Y and the sound of W by V, as with Latin; it generally has been restricted to the KJV and is felt not to represent either the Jewish or Christian tradition and texts.

In the Bible we find that El is used with modifiers a great deal to describe what kind of God, or a property or characteristic of God. The word El originated in the early Semitic language as a generic term for deity or god, used interchangeably with Baal, until the Israelites came into contact with the Canaanite religion. In early texts we learn that in Genesis 32:22-32 God is not directly named, and some argue that this reinforces the theory that YHWH did not appear as a personal name for God, until used by Moses at the time of the Exodus.

The following is a partial list of names of God:

El Elyon: Exalted one; Genesis 14:18-20

El Shaddai: God Almighty; Genesis 4:26

El Olam: God of Eternity; Genesis 21:33

El Bethel: God of Bethel; Genesis 35:7

Baal-Berith: God of Sechem Covenant; Judges 8:33, 9:4

El Berith: God of the Covenant; Judges 9:46

El Roi: God who sees me; Genesis 16:13

El Elohe-Israel: El the God of Israel; Genesis 33:19-20

Rock: Isaiah 30:29, Genesis 49:24

The First and the Last; Isaiah 44:6, 48:12

Alternate interpretations of El Bethel are "god named Bethel" and "God revealed at the shrine of Bethel". Other names of God in the Bible are; Father, Brother, Kinsman, King, Judge, Shepherd, and "living God". In Hebrew we find Yah, Yo, and Yahu. The latter was used for happy exultation and reminds one of the American cowboys yahoo (connection?). The term Elohim was generally used for Gods and gods and in most cases the singular case Eloah was used for God. <u>In discussion with a Jewish scholar he insisted there was only one name for God. YHWH.</u>

Early Christian Theology About Angels up to 451AD

As the council of Chalcedon (451AD) Origen stated in his "de Princip provem," that the early Church did not lay down definite doctrine in respect to angels, but asserted their existence. He did state that the

Church defined their nature of service as ministers of God for purposes of promoting salvation in men. Early apologists such as Justin, Tatian, Athenagoras, and Irenaeus were concerned with angels and their nature. To quote from "I Apol. p6" of Justin; "But both Him (Father) and the Son who came forth from Him and taught us these things and the host of the other good angels, who follow and are made like unto Him, and the prophetic Spirit we worship and adore". Justin inserted angels into the persons of the trinity. Several other writers even used Angel as the title of the Son. Justin's writings also identify the angel's fall as outlined in the apocryphal writings and named the demons that developed from the fallen angels and heathen gods. This followed Greek poetry and mythology as repeated by Athenagoras in Apol. 24.

Irenaeus refuted the angelology of the Gnostics and ventured that the angels are incorporeal beings, in opposition to the Gnostics, and the Christian gains nothing by invoking angels. He also discussed the fall of the angels, domination by Satan, and deliverance of man from Satan's power.

Hermas note the concept of the guardian angel, and this was reiterated by Origen partially on the basis of Deuteronomy 32:8.   Although there are several Biblical instances of angels acting as protectors that are undisputed, Origen happened to choose a passage that reads, "sons of God" in Greek and "sons of Israel" in Hebrew. Thus the foundation of his argument is in doubt. Origen went on to argue that individuals had guardian angels and that angels were invisible officers of the Church like bishop, etc..

Later Greek writers (Cappadocian Fathers) such as Basil, Gregory of Nazianzen, and Gregory of Nyssa differed in their writings, concerning the nature of angels. However, Basil states angels are more resistant to sin than man but not incapable of sin, and points Lucifer as proof. Basil discussed guardian angels also. Gregory of Nyssa had views in complete agreement with Hermas who proposed that man not only had a good angel but a bad angel also!

The early Latin Fathers such as Tertullian discuss a number of references to spirits, both good and evil. He also gives descriptions of angels blessing the baptismal water, marriages, and preparing the way for the Holy Spirit prior to baptism. He describes angels recording sin from heaven, and the fall of the angels of their own accord, the origin of a race of demons with Satan as chief. Demons were described as the source of all diseases, disasters, and bad things.

Lactantius stated that God produced a spirit in which the Divine origin did not remain and it became infected with evil and it developed to the being called Satan. He wen on to describe the Logos as the right hand of God and Satan at the left.

Later Latin Fathers such as Jerome and Ambrose essentially agreed to spirits being incorporeal beings probably created before the material world, but they differed as to the meaning of Genesis 6.

Augustine discussed angels in some length and considered them quite important. He proposed that angels minister to Christ the Head and Body (followers) on Earth. He also argued that angels ascend and descend between heaven and Earth, and that they received the grace of God at their creation. His position was that the "sons of God" in Genesis were not angels. He also supported Basil's argument that the sin of the angels which caused them to fall was pride and Augustine added the sin of envy; envy of God. Augustine stated that the evil angels were used by God to chastise the wicked, punish the good for their faults, and to test men. He stated the evil angels deceive men. Augustine did not believe in guardian angels or assert that they should be worshipped.

Early Christian Theology About Angels 451AD to 800AD

The period of 451AD to 800AD was a period of trouble experienced because some people were worshipping angels and praying to angels. Canon 35 of the Council of Laodicea forbade Christians "to forsake the Church of God, and go away and name angels, and to form assemblied, which is unlawful."

Theodoret noted that worship of angels was a special problem in Phrygia and Pisidia. Pagan people of the time criticized the Church for worshipping beings other than God. Churches were dedicated to angels after 800AD. It is believed that the Second Council of Nicea (787AD) gave the cult of the angels official recognition. Around 500AD, an account by pseudo-Dionysius detailed the rank and hierarchy of angels from nearest God to man, which was supported by Gregory the Great, later.

Early Christian Theology About Angels fro 800AD to the Reformation

From 800AD to the Reformation good and evil spirits are discussed a great deal and generally followed the thought of Augustine. The hierarchy of angels was favored and became quite popular when John Scotus Erigena translated the "Aeropagite". Canon 1 of the fourth Lateran Council (1215AD) stated among other things that, "God is the Creator of all things visible and invisible, spiritual, and corporeal. The devil and other demons were created, indeed, good by God, and became bad of their own accord (per se). Man sinned by suggestion of the devil".

Theologians of the time differed with the decree, especially the part that said the devil had guardian angels for himself. There was general agreement that good men and sinners had guardian angels. It was thought that evil spirits tempted and incited man, approaching man through his lower nature because evil spirits do not have the power to affect the free will or spiritual knowledge. Areas of dispute at the time were; substance, essence, endowments of grace, peccability, and individuation of angels.

The first systematic theologian of the Western Church was probably Peter Lombard (circa 1160AD) and he discussed good and evil spirits, their creation, free will, angel's fall, relation of demons to angels, angel's relation to magic, and whether or not Michael, Raphael, and Gabriel were individual spirits or orders of spirits. Anselm rejected the old theory man was made to fill out the number of angels and he stated that man was made for himself not to replace individuals of another nature. Anselm admitted to the dissenting opinion.

From Thomas Aquinas's "Tractatus de Angelis" quoted by Hastings; "Angels are altogether incorporeal, not composed of matter and form, exceed corporeal beings in number just as they exceed them in perfection; differ in species since they differ in rank; and are incorruptible because they are immaterial. Angels can assume an aerial body but do not exercise functions of life. Thus they do not eat proprie as Christ did after His resurrection. Angels can be localized but cannot be in more than one place at the same time. The substance of angels is not pure thought, because, in a created being, activity and substance are never identical. Similarly the esse of angels is not pure thought. They have no sensory cognition. The cognition is objective........not, however, through determinations in the object but through innate categories. The cognition of higher angels is effected by simpler and fewer categories than is that of the lower. Angels by their natural powers have knowledge of God far greater than man can have, but imperfect in itself. They have limited knowledge of future events. The angels are possessed of will, which differs from the intellect in that, while they have knowledge of good and evil, their will is only in the direction of good. Their will is free, and they are devoid of passion. The angels are not co-eternal with God, but were created by Him ex niholo at a point in time (this is strictly de fide); their creation was not prior to that of the material world (the contrary opinion is her permitted). The angels were created in a state of natural, not super-natural beatitude. Although they could love God as their Creator, they were incapable of beatific vision except by Divine grace. They are capable of acquiring merit, whereby perfect beatitude is attained; subsequently to its attainment they are incapable of sin. The beatitude being perfected, they are incapable of progress."

Concerning evil spirits Aquinas taught that the devil desired to be as God and that no demons are naturally evil, but all fall by the exercise of their own free will. The fall of the devil was not simultaneous with his creation, otherwise God would be the cause of evil.

Therefore, Aquinas argued, there was an interval between creation and the fall of the demons (angels). He also argued that the devil was originally the greatest of all the angels and that his sin was the cause of other fallen angels by incitement but not by compulsion. Less angels have fallen than have persevered. The minds of the demons are obscured by the deprivation of knowledge. He said that just as good angels are fixed in their goodness after beatification, the evil angels are fixed in the direction of evil. The demons suffer pain which is not of a sensory nature, and they have a double abode; hell where they torture the damned and the air where they incite men to evil.

The Protestant theologians of the Reformation retained good and evil spirits and their intercession for mankind. They did not believe in any worshipping of spirits.

According to Hastings there was a lot of discussion among Protestant theologians during the 18th century concerning angels, but in a "philosophic and idealizing" sense to quote a phrase from Hagenbach. The modern Christian church does not seem to have any real excitement on the subject (again, Hastings), although subtle changes have taken place in the Roman Catholic church.

Evil

It is easy to see from the preceding that when the origin of the angels is discussed, the origin of the demons has to be addressed and the origin of evil.

For approximately 1700 years, according to one source, the Christian tended to think of evil as the result of some diabolical activity. The argument is that this idea was fostered by Clement of Rome, by his misunderstanding of Canaanite mythology.

Allegedly, he did not have enough background to know, at that time, that the OT references in Canaanite mythology to opposers of God were human kings, not superhuman beings. That is not to say there is no devil from this argument, but does imply that Clement read something into the source that was not there. I believe that many Christians think of themselves being overcome by some superhuman being and taken into evil, which is different from being incited to evil.

In this theme we have seen many references to the Bible and evil used repeatedly to describe a number of events directly connected to God, and we ask an age old question, "How can God be evil?". Before we even try to give some classical answers to that question, the word evil will be examined to some extent.

In the Bible are evil spirits, lying spirits, destroying spirits, and various "evil" events caused by God, especially as chastisement, punishment, or as a test. Hastings argues that an evil spirit or even noted in the Bible, does not have to be morally evil. For example, the event might be very ill or evil to the man or men involved, but that does not mean morally evil. If it did, we have to accept that God was directly involved with morally evil events which is unacceptable.

The event of David being incited to take a census is recorded in 1 Chronicles 21:1 as, "Satan stood up against Israel, and incited David to number Israel." While the same even in 2 Samuel 24:1 reads, "Again the anger of the Lord was kindled against Israel, and he incited David against them, saying "Go, number Israel and Judah." We must either believe that Lactantius was right about God being good and evil, or review our interpretation of the word of satan, which means oppose or hinder. The word and phrase in 1 Chronicles is read in several translations as the Opposer instead of Satan. This would imply that a supernatural being we in opposition or opposed to the Israelites at that time, which is satisfactorily explained by 2 Samuel.

It is stated that God is accused of being evil directly in the Bible if read literally. In Exodus 32:14 and 1 Chronicles 32:21 a human man rebukes God and God reverses His stand, which is stated as saying the God repented of His evil. The only acceptable understanding of this phrase again must return to the context, where God has been testing and chastising His people. The people of that time had to connect all events, good and bad back to their God and all bad events were evil. That God took mercy and stopped His punishment is understandable, but not that he repented of evil.

A further demonstration of the early peoples desire to link all events and happenings back to God is in Isaiah 45:6-7, Amos 3:6, and 1 John 4:4. The writings in Isaiah and Amos are believed to be attempts by the authors to bring the Jewish people back to the conception of pre-exilic times. The passage in Isaiah reads that God creates evil in KJV and woe in RSV; the latter phrase probably better describing man's feeling of punishment or chastisement. We know that God temps man from many places in the Bible. Most of these references read temptation rather than test, except in the most modern translations. The Lord's Prayer (Matthew 6:9) in RSV reads partially, "And lead us not into temptation," where in the NEB the same line reads, "And to not bring us to the test, ".

Late News on the Lord's Prayer from BBC News

(I must add a 8 December 2017 suggestion by Pope Francis to change the wording to "do not let us fall into temptation". It is a translation from the Latin

Vulgate a 4th century Latin translation which itself was translated from ancient Greek, Hebrew, and Aramaic.

Back to my 1968 writing:

I believe that Christ's own teaching would not imply that God tempts us in our modern concept of the word which carries the connotation of moral evil. Better yet, and more understandable would be Christ interceding for man and asking God not to test us as frail humans; knowing what happened to Job for example.

Some early thought on evil

There is much unanimity among those were Duns Scotus, Thomas Aquinas, and Augustine. The Fourth Lateran Council (1215AD) stated in part; "For the devil, and other demons were created good by nature, by God, but of their own doing they became evil".

It also stated that the devil rules hell and is therefore responsible for it. Pope Pius XIII added that since angels are personal beings, therefore demons are personal beings.

Leibniz stated metaphysical evil by saying our existence as less than perfect makes us evil, of which the counter argument is that we are not created angels, but nothing prevents us from becoming angels. Physical evil exists in the form of moral pain or sorrow, psychoses, neuroses, and the like. Voltaire argued that natural events such as typhoons, hurricanes, etc. are not by Divine providence but admitted they cause suffering. Moral evil or sin is a privation affecting free will, or evil is a voluntary perversion for a Christian. A number of men such as Descartes, Leibniz, Kant, and Malbauche are quoted as agreeing to the statement; "God is the single principle of the world, a principle infinitely good and wise. Evil does not come from Him, but arises from a lapse of will."

Augustine argued that the fall of man in Genesis by eating the forbidden fruit was the start of evil. Some people have argued however, that presence of the serpent and fruit suggest a prior evil. Thus, Manicheaus argued that God made man capable of sin and is therefore responsible. Augustine's answer is a classic in my opinion and the best found in this search. He said that free will is perfection and thus God made man in perfection and man chose wrongly, therefore sinning. I believe Augustine implies that making man in His image God had to give him free will.

To continue with Augustine's line of reasoning let us quote here, "God allows evil to enter into this order……..not as essential to order, since evil is directly willed…..but accidentally, in virtue of the needs of mercy, of wisdom, and of Divine power. All this is to say that God makes suffering serve a purpose. Suffering would be absurd if it were useless, if it did not atone for sin, or become the condition for a good. For by sin, man can know his misery, humble himself before God, and seek His help. In this way, Divine providence is absolved from blame for evil……if there is a mystery, nonetheless there is no injustice". You may not choose to accept Augustine's reasoning completely, but it is difficult to find an equally all inclusive address of God, evil, and human suffering in such brevity and spiritual depth.

Some general comments

From some of the above references and our Bible we see that man has struggled considerably with the question of, "why evil?". As stated in 2 Thessalonians 2:7 the evil or lawlessness is a mystery.

However, I believe that too many Christians, including myself, have failed to examine ourselves in the same light as our early Church Fathers. I believe that we have tended to transfer, through mythology, apocryphal influences, and wishful thinking that the NT references (page 27) to the devil as prince of the world have relieved us of responsibility. I believe that it is plain to see that the devil could only be prince of "worldly conformity" to paraphrase Romans 12:2. We as men must realize that our free will is a virtuous gift, not to be abused, and that the works of the devil were destroyed by Christ as told in 1 John 3:8. In other words, I tend to agree with the

Rabbi I discussed the devil with. He did not believe in a supernatural competitor of God's for men's souls (not all Christians do but some give that impression). He said, "There is a little beast in all of us, isn't there?"

No matter what your view it should be clear that God's providence provided for reconciliation through his Grace, which was announced shortly after the fall in Genesis 3:15.

John 3:16-17 "God loved the world so much that he gave his only Son, that everyone who has faith in him may not die but have eternal life.

See also Psalm 54 and James 1:12-15